DAVID CAUSEY

A Life in Music

by

Greg Causey

© 2021   ISBN: 978-1-946766-60-1

Published by Romance Divine LLC

Note from the author: This book used original source material: newspaper clippings and photos. Many of these were decades old and showed definite aging. Various digital techniques and enhancements were used to render these items as clear as possible for print publication. In a few instances a photo or two had to be rejected because of its poor original quality. Some photos in the book made the transition to print better than others. I included as many as possible in order to pay tribute to that cadre of talented Decatur musicians. They deserve to be remembered.

Greg Causey, 2021

INTRODUCTION

This is the story of David. No, not *that* David, the David of the Bible. This is the story of Decatur, Illinois native and musician David Causey, my Uncle. However, like the David of the Bible, who played the lyre and sang songs, David Causey played the guitar and sang songs. In fact, as of the writing of this book in 2021, he still does play guitar and sing for himself and friends.

David was an early influence on my own fledging musical career. I can remember going to my Grandparents house on 16th street in Decatur and seeing his guitar and amplifier. Sometimes the other band members would leave their equipment there as well; it was quite something for a young teenager to see.

He gave me my first blues albums: Lightnin' Hopkins *Live at the Bird Lounge* and *Southern' Meetin'* by Sonny Terry and Brownie McGee. That started me on a lifelong appreciation of Blues, which led to Jazz. I still have those albums, fifty four years later.

David, or Dave to his friends, has a long musical history in Decatur, fronting Decatur's first rock and roll band, *The Headhunters* in the 50's, to the *Trambones* who played dates with the Elvis Presley band, and to being the rhythm guitarist and vocalist for the popular dance band, *The Blue Notes*, into the 70s. His musical sojourn also took him to South Bend, Indiana for a while and he spent a year playing bass guitar in a Surf band in southern California at the beginning of the surf movement in the early 60s. From fronting Decatur's first Rock band to playing in a Surf band in southern California, David really was on the forefront of many musical first waves. This book is my own attempt to honor my Uncle's musical career, and that of the musicians, many from Decatur, he played with.

The photos came from my Uncle's own collection and a few that I had. I have attempted to research and document as much information as I can, but the story goes back sixty plus years and things do get sketchy: people pass, buildings are torn down, things get lost or destroyed. Any errors, misinformation or misspelling of names may be attributed to the author.

Many of the early black and white photos were taken by a photographer friend of David's, Charlie Stockton, who followed the band and documented many of the bands early moments in black and white.

And thanks to David's friend, Kenny Duggar, who said, "We should do a book about Dave's music."

We did.

Gregory Causey, 2021

In the Beginning...

David can easily tell you the first time he was bitten by the music bug. He said he was probably twelve years old and was out collecting for his paper route on a drizzly day. To get out of the rain he ducked into a music store on 16th street, he believes it was called The Music Box.

When he went inside he saw three men playing music. There was an upright bass player and a drummer playing with brushes. But what really caught his eye was the man, Gil Voss, playing the large, blonde acoustic archtop guitar. David was entranced as the trio played standard ballads and knew he wanted to do *that*. Play the guitar. Make music.

He started out on ukulele with a device that attached to the ukulele neck with rubber bands and had buttons you pressed to make the chords. Armed with that and an Arthur Godfrey songbook he began his musical odyssey. People younger than fifty can Google Arthur Godfrey and what is 'collecting' for a paper route.

Ukulele, banjo and then guitar started him on his path and then came the birth of rock and roll. David was ready and formed what was arguably Decatur's first rock band: *The Headhunters*.

The rest, as they say, is history. David continued to play music in Decatur and central Illinois, South Bend, Indiana and in Southern California. Throughout his career he has played standards, rock and country in bars, nightclubs and for large dances. If you ask him, he'd tell you he wouldn't change a thing.

David performing a song at an office party at *The Blue Mill*. 1954-55?

It looks like he's playing a Harmony acoustic guitar.

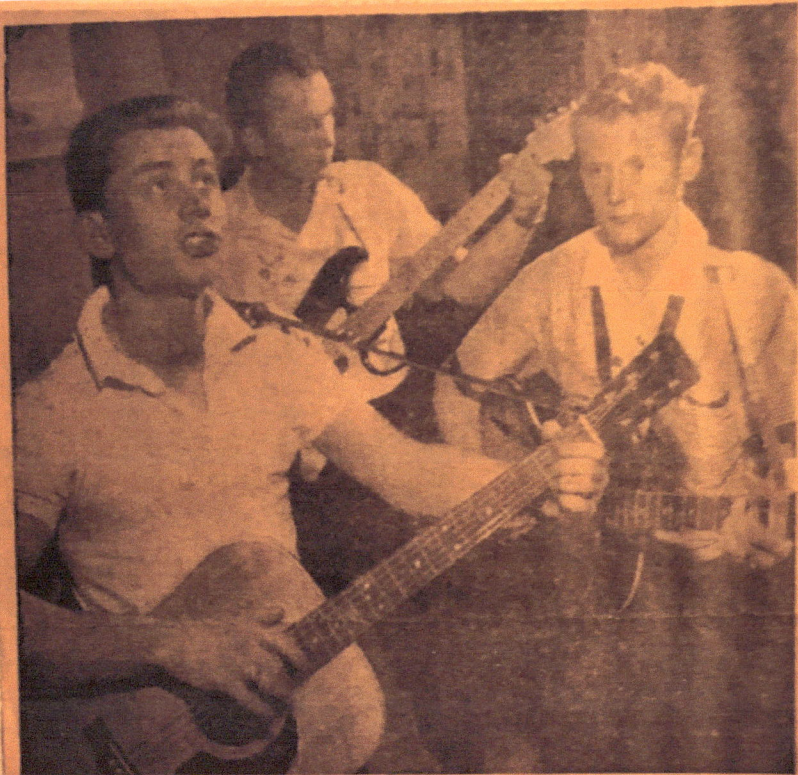

"The Headhunters," a teen-age rock 'n roll combo including from left, Dave Causey, vocalist, Paul Foster and Dick Alumbaugh belt out a number to be featured in the Fun Fair variety shows June 13 and 14.

(Herald and Review Photo)

Fun Fair Committees Announce Acts For Hospital Benefit Variety Shows

Fun Fair variety shows to be presented at matinee and evening performances June 13 and 14 at Fairview Park will open with a medley of show tunes presented by Ed Bryant, vocalist from Stephen Decatur High School. Opening with the traditional "Show Business," the medley will include numbers from hit musicals through the years.

Other acts to appear on the benefit programs are:

Barbara Sue Gillespie, baton

Dot 'n Dash square dance group with Gail Quick as caller

and Mrs. Charlene Haws as manager.

Variety of dance numbers by students at the Jacqueline Robertson School of Dancing.

Ann Meeks, vocalist

Martha Van Hook, vocalist with Larry Boerner, accompanist

The Headhunters, rock 'n roll combo

Other acts will be announced at a later date.

The Fun Fair is sponsored jointly by the auxiliaries of Decatur and Macon County and St. Mary's Hospital.

While still in high school, David formed his first rock and roll 'combo' *The Headhunters*. The name came from the shrunken heads they often displayed from the head stocks of their guitars (for those that remember fuzzy dice and shrunken heads hanging from rear view mirrors).

They performed at several of the local YWCA Fun Fairs, at Fairview Park and John's Hill Park.

David believes this picture is from 1957 (?).

Left to right in the picture are David Causey, Paul Foster and Dick Alumbaugh.

David often had a female Alto Sax player from Maroa perform with the group. Her name was Roxie Gray. David said she was quite talented and decades later would sometimes perform with him in *The Blue Notes*.

GEAR NOTES

David is playing an early D-28 Martin guitar. He said he paid $105 for it from a man he said worked at the local A&P grocery store. In 2020, these guitars were selling for $20,000 dollars or more, depending on condition.

Paul Foster is playing an early Fender Stratocaster. 1957 versions have been known to sell for $20,000 to $50,000, depending on condition, finish and other variables.

Dick Alumbaugh is playing a Gibson ES-125. These currently sell for around $2,500.

At top, Hap Jensen, center, master of ceremonies for WSOY's Saturday night jam session, and his two platter spinners, Jean McEvoy, left, and Mike Cheever, have themselves a belly laugh. Below, the "Quarter Notes," Charlotte Weatherholt, at left, Linda Tate, Nancy King and Lona Beggs blend in melody with Eddie McCarty at the piano. The two guitar strummers are Allen Sparks and Dave Causey. When things get rolling the kids start rocking, and the girl in this couple took her shoes off to dance. Seated in the end picture are three spectators, laughing at the festivities in Studio C. Sometimes

David Causey playing on local radio station WSOY. Accompanying him on guitar is Allen "Sparky" Sparks. David said Sparky was a year older and could play really good rock guitar. David and Sparky would often play together until around 1959. The DJ is Pat Jensen.

David said he played at the radio station a few times and on Saturday mornings they would sometimes go and play on WHOW in Clinton.

He also played on WDZ, downtown Decatur on South Park Street. It was the announcer at WDZ, Marty Roberts, who put David and his group in touch with the Elvis Presley band when they toured the area. David and his band did a three performance engagement with the Presley band.

Another picture of David and 'Sparky'. This one is taken at the house on 16th Street where David grew up. This picture gives a nice view of Sparky's vintage National Town and Country guitar. David is playing his Martin D-28.

'Sparky' was eventually drafted and went to Korea.

David playing with his band: *The Headhunters*.

Left to Right: Alan Martin, Upright Bass; Dick Alumbaugh, guitar; Jerry Antrum, drums; David Causey, guitar & vocals and Paul Foster, guitar.

David said Alan Martin was a good bass player, could play both upright and Fender Precision bass and also played in the school orchestra. David, Alan Martin and Dick Alumbaugh sometimes worked as a trio at the Belvedere on Water Street in Decatur. All three had early Fender Bassman amps. David was impressed with the way Alan used a bow on his electric bass when the group played *Since I Fell for You*.

Photo by Charlie Stockton

GEAR NOTES

The guitarist on the right, Paul Foster, is playing a Fender Stratocaster that was purchased by David in 1958, for $250 with case. If we only had a time machine and a handful of cash!

Dick Alumbaugh is playing his Gibson ES-125 and David is playing his Martin D-28.

They are all playing through David's Gibson GA-6 amplifier, a design that was very much like the Fender Tweed Deluxe of the time.

GEAR NOTES

David still has the receipts for the Fender Stratocaster and Gibson GA-6 amplifier he bought back in 1958. He quickly grew to dislike the Strat, saying it was hard to keep in tune. He eventually traded the Strat for Alumbaugh's Gibson ES-125. Thus began David's long love affair with Gibson archtops as he moved through the ES-125 to an ES-330 (which he still has) and to an ES-175, which he played a lot with *The Blue Notes*.

Photo by Charlie Stockton

Champaign County Fair 1958

David and his band, now called *The Trambones*, played at the Champaign County Fair in 1958. Also on the bill were *'Blue Suede Shoes'* legend Carl Perkins and a young Brenda Lee.

David got to meet and talk to Carl Perkins saying he was both talented and a gentleman.

The Trambones at the time included:

David Causey: Guitar and Vocals
Dick Alumbaugh: Guitar
Nelson 'Smitty' Smith: Drums
Allen 'Sparky' Sparks: Guitar

The Trambones at the Champaign County Fair

Left to Right: Allen 'Sparky' Sparks, guitar; Dick Alumbaugh, guitar and David Causey, guitar and vocals. Not shown: Nelson 'Smitty' Smith: drums.

GEAR NOTES:

'Sparky' has traded his National Town and Country in on a red Gretsch. Dick Alumbaugh is playing a Stratocaster. David is playing a Gibson ES-125. Dave traded his Fender Strat for Alumbaugh's Gibson ES-125.

14

Photo by Charlie Stockton

Pictured at left: Nelson 'Smitty' Smith.

While David played with many drummers over his career, he had a long association with Nelson 'Smitty' Smith.

Both drummer 'Smitty', and guitarist and bassist Paul Foster, left Decatur to find their paths crossing with other notable musicians.

Smitty played for a while with Willie Nelson before returning to Decatur.

Paul Foster moved west, to Arizona, and joined forces in Phoenix with a young Waylon Jennings, playing bass on some of Waylon's early club gigs.

Standing in the background is Johnny Barton, the DJ for WHOW.

David also worked with and appeared on the radio with Pat Jensen from WSOY; Marty Roberts at WDZ and also at WTMD in Taylorville.

Photo by Charlie Stockton

Left to Right: Allen Sparks, Dick Alumbaugh, David Causey.

This is another picture of *The Trambones* at the Champaign County Fair.

The individual just off Dick Alumbaugh's left shoulder is Johnny Barton, DJ at WHOW radio.

GEAR NOTES

This picture provides a better view of David's (formerly Dick Alumbaugh's) Gibson ES-125. David eventually traded the guitar in for a brand new 1959 Gibson ES-330. He said the ES-125 is one guitar he wishes he still had, saying it was an excellent rhythm guitar.

David is still using his Gibson GA-6 amplifier, but eventually he would buy a used 1959 5F6A Fender Bassman.

It looks as if 'Sparky' may be playing his red Gretsch through a tweed Fender amp on a chair.

In 1959, with Elvis Presley in the U.S. Army, his former backup band was on the road and touring. Their travels took them to the Decatur area where they performed three shows in Tuscola, Springfield and at the 101 Ranch Park. David and his band *The Trambones* were on the bill for all three engagements. This picture shows the band playing their set at the Springfield Knights of Columbus.

Left to Right: Dick Alumbaugh, David Causey and Allen Sparks.

Photo by Charlie Stockton

Photo by Charlie Stockton

David playing his Gibson ES-125 at the Springfield, Illinois, Knights of Columbus in 1959. The Elvis Presley band was on the same bill. In the background is guitarist Dick Alumbaugh playing his Fender Stratocaster.

Allen 'Sparky' Sparks (left) playing a Gretsch and Dick Alumbaugh (right) playing a Fender Stratocaster at the Springfield, Knights of Columbus show with the Elvis Presley band. David said that Sparky was a good all around guitar player, but excelled on Country styles. Dick Alumbaugh came from more of a Blues and R&B background. Together, they melded well into the *Trambones* early rock style.

Photo by Charlie Stockton

The Elvis Presley Band at the Springfield, Illinois, Knights of Columbus. 1959

Left to Right: Scotty Moore (playing his blonde Gibson Super 400), Reggie Young (playing a sunburst Gibson archtop), Joe Lee on Tenor Sax, Bill Black (playing what is probably a Fender Precision Bass). Not shown (behind Reggie Young), D.J. Fontana on drums. Thomas Wayne was the featured vocalist.

The ELVIS PRESLEY Band

Scotty Moore: Scott "Scotty" Moore III (December 27, 1931 – June 28, 2016) was an American guitarist and recording engineer who formed The Blue Moon Boys in 1954, Elvis Presley's backing band. He was studio and touring guitarist for Presley between 1954 and 1968. Rock critic Dave Marsh credits Moore with inventing power chords, on the 1957 Presley song "Jailhouse Rock", the intro of which Moore and drummer D.J. Fontana, according to the latter, "copped from a '40s swing version of 'The Anvil Chorus'." Moore was ranked 29th in Rolling Stone magazine's list of 100 Greatest Guitarists of All Time in 2011. He was inducted into the Rock and Roll Hall of Fame in 2000, the Musicians Hall of Fame and Museum in 2007, and the Memphis Music Hall of Fame in 2015. (Source: Wikipedia)

Reggie Grimes Young Jr. (December 12, 1936 – January 17, 2019) was an American musician who was lead guitarist in the American Sound Studio house band, The Memphis Boys, and was a leading session musician. He played on various recordings with artists such as Elvis Presley, Joe Tex, Merrilee Rush, B.J. Thomas, John Prine, Dusty Springfield, Herbie Mann, J.J. Cale, Dionne Warwick, Roy Hamilton, Willie Nelson, Waylon Jennings, the Box Tops, Johnny Cash, Jerry Lee Lewis, Merle Haggard, Joey Tempest, George Strait, and The Highwaymen. Young was inducted into the Musicians Hall of Fame and Museum in 2019. (Source: Wikipedia)

William Patton Black Jr. (September 17, 1926 – October 21, 1965) was an American musician and bandleader who is noted as one of the pioneers of rock and roll. He was the bassist in Elvis Presley's early trio. Black later formed Bill Black's Combo. Black played on early Presley recordings including "Good Rockin' Tonight", "Heartbreak Hotel", "Baby Let's Play House", "Mystery Train", "That's All Right", and "Hound Dog", and eventually became one of the first bass players to use the Fender Precision Bass (bass guitar) in popular music, on "Jailhouse Rock", in the late 1950s. (Source: Wikipedia)

Thomas Wayne, born Thomas Wayne Perkins, was the brother of Johnny Cash's guitarist, Luther Perkins. He released several singles between 1958 and 1964, primarily on the labels Fernwood and Mercury, including "This Time", which would later become a hit for Troy Shondell. He scored a major U.S. hit with the song "Tragedy" (credited to Thomas Wayne with the DeLons), which peaked at #20 on the R&B Singles chart and #5 on the Billboard Hot 100 in 1959. It sold over one million copies, earning gold disc status. The song proved to be his only hit, however. Later, Wayne worked as a sound engineer, before he died in a car accident, at the age of 31, in Memphis in 1971. (Source: Wikipedia)

Dominic Joseph Fontana (March 15, 1931 – June 13, 2018) was an American musician best known as the drummer for Elvis Presley for 14 years. In October 1954 he was hired to play drums for Presley, which marked the beginning of a fifteen-year relationship. He played on over 460 RCA cuts with Elvis. (Source: Wikipedia)

ELVIS-PRESLEY-PLATZ

Elvis Aron Presley, ✳ 8.Januar 1935 † 16. August 1977,
war vom 1. Oktober 1958 bis zum 2. März 1960 als Soldat
in den Ray Barracks in Friedberg stationiert.
In Bad Nauheim wohnte er zunächst in Hilberts Parkhotel,
dann im Hotel Grunewald und schließlich in der Goethestraße 14

Photo by Greg Causey

Photo by Greg Causey

A Note from the Author: My wife and I lived and worked in Germany for six years, from 1997 to 2003. I took these pictures of the way the people of *Bad Nauheim* honored their famous visitor. The *Elvis Presley Platz* is their designation for what we would call a town *square*. The people of *Bad Nauheim* are quite proud of their association with Elvis and many monuments to him can be seen around the town. The plaque above reads: From October 1, 1958 to March 2, 1960, Elvis Presley was stationed as a soldier in the Ray Barracks in *Friedberg*. In *Bad Nauheim* he initially lived in *Hilbert's Parkhotel*, then in the *Hotel Grunewald* at *Goethestrasse* 14.

Here is another monument to Elvis in *Bad Nauheim*. You can see that even in the '90's, people are still leaving flowers.

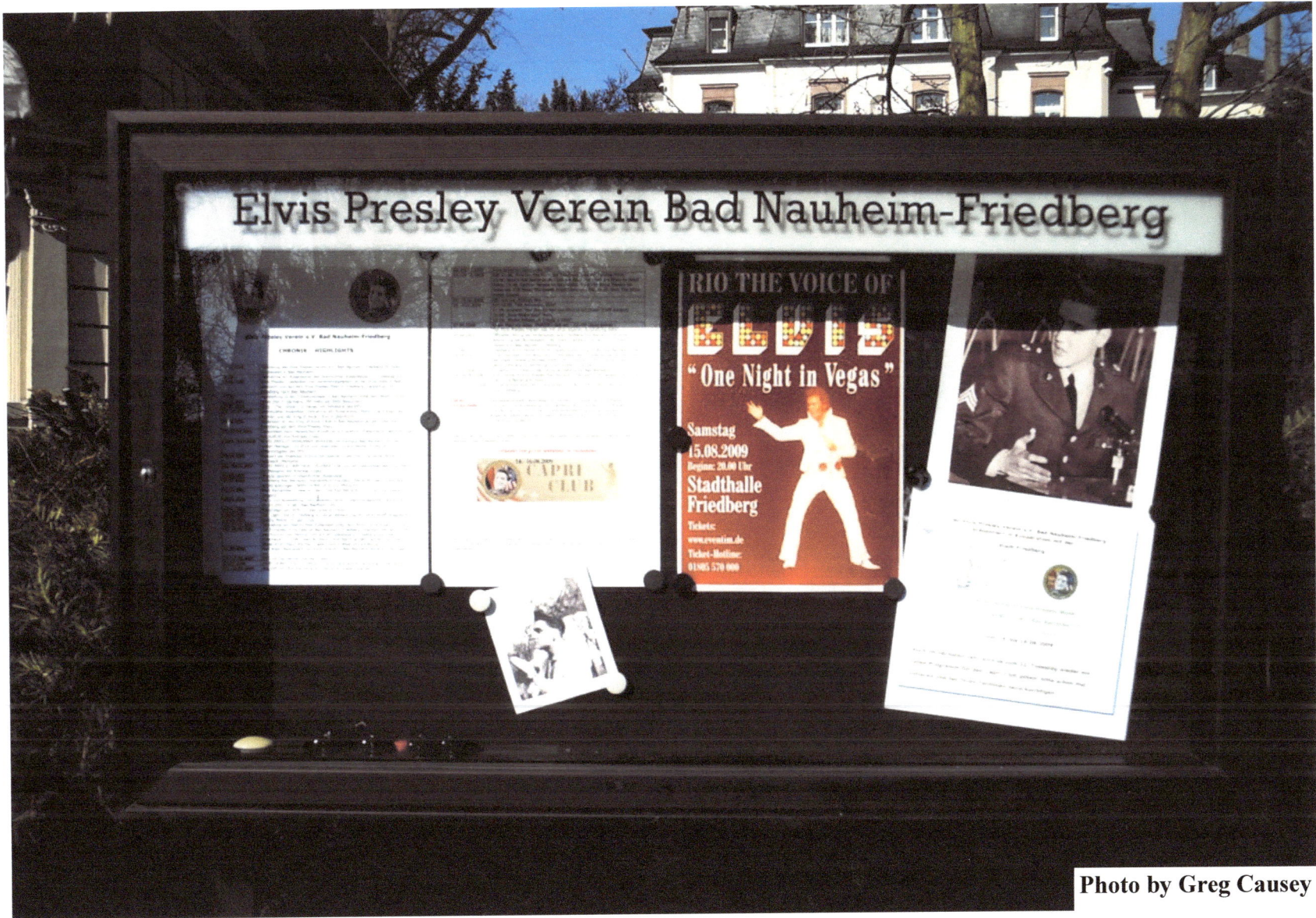

Photo by Greg Causey

This is a street exhibit from the local Elvis Presley *Verein Bad Nauheim-Friedberg*, which is the local 'Elvis Presley Society'. You can see there is a flyer for a show by a local Elvis impersonator on *Samstag* (Saturday).

The last engagement with the Presley Band was on a Sunday at Spitler Woods at the 101 Ranch Park (now a housing development).

Left to Right: Nelson 'Smitty' Smith on drums, Dick Alumbaugh on guitar, David Causey on guitar and vocals and Allen 'Sparky' Sparks on guitar.

The Trambones at 101 Ranch Park

Left to Right: Nelson 'Smitty' Smith, drums; Dick Alumbaugh, guitar, David Causey, guitar and vocals and Allen 'Sparky' Sparks, guitar.

The Trambones at 101 Ranch Park

Left to Right: Nelson 'Smitty' Smith, drums; Dick Alumbaugh, guitar, David Causey, guitar and vocals and Allen 'Sparky' Sparks, guitar.

GEAR NOTES: David is singing through two microphones, maybe old Shure 55s (?). It looks like there is perhaps a Fender tweed on the chair and Sparky may be playing through a small Gibson amp.

26

Photo by Charlie Stockton

Photo by Charlie Stockton

Left: Drummer Nelson 'Smitty' Smith. Right: David Causey at 101 Ranch Park at Spitler Wood. David and Smitty were close friends, Smitty often introducing David to people as his *brother*.

Paul Foster playing a Fender Precision bass.

Paul was skilled on both bass and guitar and played often with David on both instruments.

Photo by Charlie Stockton

Photo by Charlie Stockton

Allen 'Sparky' Sparks playing his Gretsch at the 101 Ranch Park.

GEAR NOTES: There are a lot of small tube amplifiers, Gibson and Fender, in these pictures. It's interesting to note that many of today's musicians have left their huge amplifier stacks behind and have returned to the sweet tone of a 'cranked' small tube amplifier. Gibson GA-6s, Skylarks, Fender Champs and Deluxes bring premium prices on today's vintage market. Sparky's Gretsch looks to be a 6120 model.

Guitarist Dick Alumbaugh playing at the 101 Ranch Park.

He's playing the Fender Stratocaster that David originally bought and later traded for Dick's ES-125.

David really liked the Gibson ES-125 and regrets trading it in when he got his brand new Gibson ES-330.

In 2017 the author bought David a Godin 5th Avenue Kingpin guitar. This is a guitar made in Canada and is very much like the ES-125 David traded away. The Godin is an archtop with F holes and a single P-90 pickup like David's beloved Gibson ES-125.

GEAR NOTES

There are several amps around Dick Alumbaugh's feet, perhaps a Gibson and tweed Fender.

It's hard to tell from the picture, but it looks like Dick's (formerly David's) Fender Strat has a two-tone sunburst finish with an obvious maple neck.

As this was a 1958 Fender, it's quite possible that the legendary Abigail Ybarra wound the pickups. "With her small hands and a resolute work ethic, Abigail found she was perfect for the skilled and meticulous work involved in winding the metal wire that was housed inside a Fender pickup, and Leo trained her himself. The last Fender guitar Abigail wired pickups for was purchased by Keith Richards of the Rolling Stones and the band Los Lobos played at her retirement party in 2013."
(Source: teachrock.org)

Photo by Charlie Stockton

Photo by Charlie Stockton

Bill Black: Bass guitarist for Elvis Presley band.

GEAR NOTES: David said he believed that Bill Black was playing a Fender Precision bass. You can see a Fender Bassman amp in the picture.

Photo by Charlie Stockton

Thomas Wayne, vocalist with the touring Elvis Presley band. He had a hit with the song *TRAGEDY*.

Elvis Presley band at 101 Ranch Park in 1959:

Left to Right: Joe Lee, tenor saxophone; Thomas Wayne, vocals, Reggie Young with guitar.

31

Elvis Presley Band 'Loading In' at the 101 Ranch Park gig in 1959.

Legendary guitarist Scotty Moore with hand on amp and Elvis's long-time drummer DJ Fontanna to the right.

The TRAMBONES and The ELVIS PRESLEY BAND at 101 Ranch Park, 1959

Standing, Left to Right: Allen 'Sparky' Sparks, Reggie Young, Thomas Wayne, Scotty Moore, DJ Fontanna, Nelson 'Smitty' Smith, David Causey Kneeling, Left to Right: Dick Alumbaugh, Bill Black, Joe Lee.

Guitarist Scotty Moore was interested in booking David's band, *The Trambones* on a club circuit in southern Alabama, Georgia and northern Florida, but the Korean War intervened and two of the band were drafted.

Left to Right: Jerry Gandy on drums. David said he was an excellent drummer who used to sub for the group. David would later work with Jerry in *The Blue Notes*. David Causey, guitar and vocals. Dick Alumbaugh, guitar. Alan Martin (?) upright bass.

GEAR NOTES: David is singing and playing his Gibson ES-125 through his Gibson GA-6 amplifier and Dick Alumbaugh is playing his Fender Stratocaster. It's hard to tell from the picture but it looks as if the microphone David is using might be a Shure Model 51.

Later in his career, David had a small combo with his first wife 'Barb' on bass and guitarist Sam Mayberry on lead guitar. The combo played rock, some blues and standards. David said Sam was a good lead guitarist, especially on standards. Sam also had a background playing with some of the local big bands. These pictures were taken at the *Western Bar* in Decatur, located at the corner of Cerro Gordo and Water Street.

GEAR NOTES:

Guitarist Sam Mayberry is playing a Les Paul with a Bigsby and P-90 pickups. Maybe he's playing through a Standel or Supro? Barb is playing a cherry red Gibson EB-O bass through David's 1959 Fender Bassman amplifier. In this picture David has traded his Gibson ES-125 for a brand new 1959 blonde Gibson ES-330 with a Bigsby.

There was seldom a time when David wasn't playing some kind of music, with someone, somewhere. In this picture he is jamming at a party on the lake with other fellow Decatur musicians.

Left to Right: David Causey, guitar and vocals; Larry Garner, guitar; Leon Broughton, accordion; Gene Eckis, bass.

Leon Broughton played with Rex Alan, the singing *Arizona Cowboy* and Gene Eckis had played on the *WLS Barndance* radio show from Chicago. David said that Gene had only his thumb and little finger on his left hand, having lost the others to an accident, but was still a good bass player.

David used to play gigs with Gene at *Dots North End Tavern* on Water Street. He also played gigs at *The Crawdad Hole* with 'Smitty' on drums, Red Burns on steel, Sam Mayberry on guitar and Red Dennison on bass.

Note: Bassist Red Dennison was a former boxer who reputedly fought Stefano "Tami" Mauriello, aka The Bronx Barkeep. Tami Mauriello lost a ten round fight with heavyweight champ Joe Louis. (Source: Wikipedia)

The *PHASE III Band* consisted of David on guitar and vocals, Loren Thompson on guitar and Dave Brubeck on bass.
 Loren Thompson was, according to David, a 'fantastic lead guitar player'.
 The band formed in the early 90s, playing together for about at year at venues such as *The Lake Lawn Lounge* and *Bluebell* in Pana.

David and his flattop entertaining friends at a party.

The BLUE NOTES

David's longest and most successful musical gig was with *The Blue Notes*, a popular and successful Decatur-based dance band. They were active from 1969 through 1980. Original members included band founder and leader Adam Fratini on accordion, David Causey on vocals and guitar, and Jim Walker on saxophone and clarinet. Various drummers played with the group over the years.

The group was founded by Adam Fratini who recruited David for the role of vocalist and rhythm guitarist. He took David out to a club one night to watch another local band. David said the other band, of Decatur musicians, was very good, all excellent players. But Adam asked how many people were dancing and David noticed that few people were actually dancing. Adam replied that the band was playing to the audience's ears and *The Blue Notes* would play to their feet. Adam had the band members take ballroom dance lessons to better acquaint them with the meters and rhythms that dancers needed. It was an astute move by a man who would become, according to David: "The smartest guy to ever run a group." David lauded Adam's skill at reading the crowd and calling out a Foxtrot, Rumba, Cha Cha, Waltz, whatever, exactly when the dancers needed a change. There was an interest in ballroom dancing at the time and *The Blue Notes* capitalized on providing live dance music. Indeed, they played for dances sponsored by dance instructors Dave and Foster Lampert who ran dance schools in Champaign and Bloomington, respectively. My parents, Dale and Jane Causey took dance classes from Dave Lampert at a place called *The Bunny Hutch* outside of Champaign, Illinois.

David was hesitant to join the group as all the other members had formal music training and David couldn't read music. A musician friend of David's heard about the new aggregation and told David he was in over his head. A few years later the man apologized and told David he had pulled it off and was now 'one of us'.

The Blue Notes were in constant demand often averaging three engagements a week and sometimes doing three in a single day! David recalled one Saturday the group played a wedding in the day at the *Holiday Inn*, a matinee at the Decatur *Country Club* and an evening dance from nine to twelve at the local *Moose Lodge*. David and Adam also held down a semi-regular weekly gig as a duo at the local *Elks Lodge*.

The group was a mainstay on the local Country Club circuit, playing venues such as the South Side Country Club, Decatur Country Club, Taylorville, Lincoln and Cresthaven Country Clubs.

The Blue Notes, left to right. David Causey, guitar and vocals; Adam Fratini, Accordion; Roger Miller, drums; Jim Walker, saxophone and clarinet. Jim Walker was the band director at Mound School and later became the president of the Decatur Municipal Band.

GEAR NOTES: David is playing his 1959 Gibson ES-330, this guitar model was a favorite of jazz guitarists Emily Remler and Grant Green, and even BB King played one for a while. He bought it new, trading his Gibson ES-125 for it. Although he liked the ES-330 and it gave him decades of service he always missed the ES-125. The group's Shure Vocal Master PA head can be seen in the background. This particular PA system was a band and club mainstay in its day. As a drummer the author played in several clubs where this was the house PA system.

From left to right: David Causey, vocals and guitar; Adam Fratini, accordion; Jim Walker, saxophone; Roger Miller, drums.

Late 1970s: David and Adam playing one of their Wednesday night duo gigs at the Elks Club.

GEAR NOTES: David is playing his Gibson ES-175. Early in his *Blue Notes* career, David played through a Heathkit TA-16 amplifier, not an amplifier you'd see on a lot of stages. The Heathkit products were build-it-yourself kits, popular with electronics hobbyists in the 60s. The TA-16 was a low powered, solid state amp with reverb and tremolo. It did, however, contain two 'Made in Chicago' twelve-inch Jensen speakers. Later he played through an Ampeg Jupiter amplifier.

The Blue Notes, looking classy in their blue jackets and black bow ties. They were a popular dance band and kept busy playing dates in many central Illinois venues. Left to right: David Causey, guitar and vocal; Adam Fratini, accordion; Terry Brennan, drums; Jim Walker, saxophone.

The drummer, Terry Brennan was a very accomplished piano player, "One of the best between Chicago and St. Louis" according to David. He was also the Warrensburg Band Director.

GEAR NOTES: It's hard to see, but David is standing in front of and playing through a 1968 Ampeg Jupiter B-22X amplifier. This is a large, and heavy, all tube amplifier, with two Jensen C12N twelve-inch speakers. David said he often had to carry this monster amp upstairs to some gigs.

David belting out a song, his big Ampeg amp behind him. David didn't have the formal musical training of the rest of the band members, but more than held up his end. The leader, Adam, once marveled at David's ability to memorize the large number of songs, the lyrics and chords, the group had in their repertoire. You'll notice there are no music stands or books of lyrics. These were real, working musicians, masters of their craft.

Left to right at a gig in Riverton, Illinois: David Causey, guitar and vocals; Adam Fratini, accordion; Jim Walker, saxophone; Jerry Gandy, drums.

GEAR NOTES: David has now acquired a 60's Gibson ES-175 guitar (he still had his original ES-330). The serial number on the guitar dates it to '1969', but some people will tell you that Gibson serial numbers can be "iffy" for dating purposes. Pot codes might be better, but I didn't want to disassemble the guitar. The guitar does have one of those smaller 60s necks, Gibson went through different neck sizes in the 60s. These smaller necks were on the 1965 - 1967 guitars, so I believe it fits somewhere in that time span. David was told it was a '65' when he bought it, so it might well be. It looks as if he is playing it through his 1959 Fender 5F6A Bassman amp (below the Vocal Master PA head). David bought the Bassman amp used in the 60s. The original tweed covering was ripped and had cigarette burns so he recovered it in a brown leather Tolex. A 60s Gibson ES-175 through a '59 Bassman, that had to sound good.

Jerry Gandy playing drums. Jerry was one of several drummers to perform with *The Blue Notes*. David said he was an "Excellent drummer" who also played with the Tiny Hill Big Band in Decatur.

Saxophonist Jim Walker. Although his main instrument was the clarinet, he was also an accomplished saxophonist. One of the original *Blue Notes* members, he seldom missed a gig. When necessary, local sax players John Diss or Roxie Gray filled in as *The Blue Notes* reed man.

The Blue Notes swinging at a Knights of Columbus dance at Riverton, Illinois. Left to right: David Causey, guitar and vocals; Adam Fertini, accordion; Jerry Gandy, drums; Jim Walker, saxophone.

GEAR NOTES: This picture gives a better look at David's Ampeg Jupiter amp and his Gibson ES-175 guitar.

David singing and playing at a *Blue Notes* gig.

Adam Fratini: the original founder and leader of *The Blue Notes.*

Clockwise from top left: Jerry Gandy, drums; Jim Walker, Saxophone; Adam Fratini, accordion; David Causey, guitar and vocals.

The author's favorite picture in the book. A classic look, a classic guitar and a man in his musical prime.

GEAR NOTES: At this gig David is playing his 1960s Gibson ES-175 guitar and his 1959 Fender Bassman amplifier (seen in the lower left corner). The Bigsby tailpiece on the guitar is something that was added on at some point. The author now has both the guitar and amp and has given the amplifier a much-needed electronic restoration. With the exception of changing the guitar's Tune-o-matic bridge for a 40s era, rosewood bridge, the guitar has had little work other than new strings, cleaning and a basic setup by a guitar tech. The guitar has finish checking, faded binding and decades worth of good playing mojo. People talk about instruments improving after they've been 'played in'. With decades of 'four-to-the-bar' rhythm chords, a wooden bridge and heavy gauge flat wound strings this guitar is a jazz monster.

The Blue Notes

Left to Right: David Causey, guitar and vocals; Adam Fratini, accordion; Tony Fratini, drums; Jim Walker, saxophone. David is playing his 1959 Gibson ES-330 through his Heathkit TA-16 amplifier.

Paul Foster (pictured above with a red Gretsch guitar) was an early musical colleagues of David's, playing both bass and guitar in some of David's early bands. He traveled west, settling in the Phoenix area, and hooked up with another guitar player and singer, Waylon Jennings. Paul played bass and did some vocals in Waylon's early breakout band at a local Phoenix hotspot called J.D.'s. Enterprising individuals can search the web and find interviews with Paul Foster as well as some tracks of the early Waylon band with Paul doing some vocals. The picture above was taken when David went out west to visit his brother, Dale, who lived in Tucson.

The picture above shows David, left with an acoustic, and Paul Foster, right, jamming at David's brother's home in Tucson during one of David's visits out west. It looks like Paul may be playing his red Gretsch.

Dave Brubeck, above, was a good friend of David's who played with him in the *Phase III Band*. While he is shown playing a guitar, he was really an electric bass player. David said he was making good progress at mastering the upright bass, when he tragically passed away too young.

THE FOUR DAYS.

Harold Kudlets Agency
45 East Avenue N.
Hamilton, Ont. Canada
Jackson 2-0900

Sweet and Salty was a local Decatur group. Among the members were John Diss, on saxophone (right) and Terry Brennan (who also played drums with *The Blue Notes*) bottom, on piano. John Diss would sometimes sub for Jim Walker in *The Blue Notes*. David used to play jobs with John Diss, Alan Martin on bass, and Dell Kirby on drums.

During his time in California, David played with the drummer Frank Rankin (above, top center) originally from Hamilton, Ontario, Canada. They played country rock and David described him as a good guy, perhaps one of the few positive things he found about life in 60s California.

Photo by Joan Causey

David Causey (left) and Greg Causey (right) jamming in David's living room in Decatur, Illinois in 2005.

GEAR NOTES: David is playing his Epiphone flattop. Greg is playing his 1993 Fender Jazzmaster through David's 1982 Fender Pro Reverb amp.

The author, Greg Causey, seated at left and David standing at right. This picture was taken in 2007 (?) at a local jam session in Moweaqua, Illinois, held at a former shoe store and re-christened *The Pickin' Palace*.

GEAR NOTES: David is playing his jumbo Epiphone flattop and Greg is playing a 2002 Collector's Edition Ovation.

In CONCLUSION

It was never the author's intention to suggest David Causey was the greatest musician to come from Decatur. That distinction would surely fall to notable Decatur musical sons and daughters such as Homer 'Boots' Randolph, June Christy, Alison Krauss and Brian Culbertson, to name but a few. Indeed, David would be the first to regale you with tales of the excellent local musicians he has played with and heard over his lifetime of music in Decatur.

But David did enjoy a decades long career as a stalwart of the local music scene. Thousands of people over the years listened to him sing and danced to his music. Even now, when you walk into his home, one can see guitars, a mandolin, amplifiers, even a banjo. Stacks of vinyl records display his musical influences and personal preferences: Perry Como, Tony Bennett, Howard Roberts, Diana Krall, Antonio Carlos Jobim and many, many others. Music has always been a large part of his life and work.

His musical success can best be measured not in downloads, 'likes', or streaming numbers, but rather in the joy he brings to himself and others when he plays his guitar and sings his songs.

The END

2018, over sixty-five years since his musical odyssey began, David sits in his home in Decatur, Illinois, strumming on a ukulele (left) and a guitar (right). His truly was, and still is: *A Life in Music*.

Photos by Kenny Duggar

About the Author

Gregory (Greg) Causey was born in Decatur, Illinois, but has moved around for his career, living in Arizona, California, Maine, Germany and Ohio. He retired from the government after thirty-plus years of working for the Department of Defense both in and out of uniform. He is a veteran of the USAF, 93rd Bomb Wing, Strategic Air Command.

Inspired by his Uncle David, music has been a large part of his life. He played drums in various bands from the 60s through the 90s, but now focuses his musical attention on guitar. After his retirement he has enjoyed ballroom dancing, writing, and of course, music.

He lives in Ohio with his wife Joan, who had an even more stellar career, retiring from the Pentagon as an SES (Senior Executive Service) level 2, the civilian equivalent of a two-star General.

Web Site: www.gregcausey.com

1970

2012

2016

The author, Greg Causey, playing drums in clubs in Flagstaff, Arizona, 1970.

GEAR NOTES: The bass player (right) is using a Mosrite bass through a Fender Showman amp with two speaker cabinets. Near his feet is a Fender Deluxe Reverb. The guitar player is playing a gold Gibson Les Paul Deluxe with mini humbuckers through a Fender Twin Reverb with JBL speakers; that was a very heavy amplifier. Greg is singing through his Shure 515S Unidyne microphone. He bought two in 1968 and still has them in 2021.

www.ingramcontent.com/pod-product-compliance
Lightning Source LLC
Chambersburg PA
CBHW040452100426

42813CB00021BA/2977